M000268296

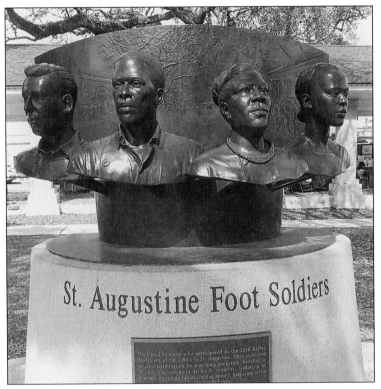

The bronze sculpture "St. Augustine Foot Soldiers," by artist Brian Owens, is located in the Plaza de la Constitución in St. Augustine, Florida. The sculpture commemorates the many brave individuals who participated in civil rights demonstrations in the city during the 1960s. The artist has depicted a white male college student, a middle-aged African American man, an older African American woman, and an African American teenage girl to represent the many different people who used nonviolent protests, such as lunch counter sit-ins, picketing at the plaza, and swimming at segregated beaches, to fight peacefully for racial equality. The demonstrators had the strength to keep their protests nonviolent, even when faced with violent opposition.

While the teenage girl in the sculpture represents many different individuals, you can imagine that she is Maggie Jefferson, the main character in this novel.

To Melissa—
Embrace your
power to change
the world!
Judy Lindquist

FORCING CHANGE

Judy Lindquist

FORCING CHANGE

Copyright © 2017 by Judy Lindquist

All characters in this book have been presented as accurately as possible through testimonies by those remaining, or from trial records and other chronicles of this time period.

In accordance with the U.S. Copyright Act of 1976, the scanning, uploading and electronic sharing of any part of this book without permission of the author constitute unlawful piracy and theft of the author's intellectual property. No part of this book may be reproduced or transmitted in any form or by any means, electronic or mechanical, including photocopying, recording, or by any information storage and retrieval system, except for excerpts used for reviews, without permission in writing from the author.

ISBN: 978-1-886104-95-2

This project is sponsored in part by the Department of State, Division of Cultural Affairs, the Florida Council of Arts and Culture and the State of Florida.

Florida Historical Society Press
435 Brevard Avenue, Cocoa, FL 32922
http://myfloridahistory.org/fhspress

PRESS

Dedication

This book is dedicated to the thousands of people in the 1950s and 1960s who selflessly put their lives on the line to stand up and defy hate and bigotry. Their nonviolent resistance, in the face of such unjust treatment, was awe inspiring. Let us never forget their sacrifices.

Chapter 1

June 26, 1963

Have you ever had a moment in your life where you looked around and wondered, "How did I get here?"

I don't mean the "where do babies come from?" question that we ask our parents—and that they always get flustered about. I mean the *"how did I end up in this situation?"* question.

Sitting here at the lunch counter with my friends, seeing the glaring look of the waitress and the manager. Hearing the crowd begin to gather behind us. Trying to keep my hands still in my lap because if I lift them up they will shake in a giveaway of how scared I really am. I am having one of those moments. Watching the manager pick up the telephone, I know exactly what he is doing. He is calling the police. I am going to be arrested.

I did not set out to get arrested. Well . . . maybe I did. But I am a good girl. I am polite. I do my chores and help out around the house. I follow my parents' directions. I do a great deal of the cooking at home and even watch my little brother when asked. I do well in school. In fact, I do so well that my teachers have already told my parents that I will be able to go to college after high school. My dream is to be a teacher, and I know I will be able to do that.

Well, I thought I could before today.

I don't know what will happen when the police arrive. Will I be put in handcuffs and dragged away? Will I be put in jail? How long would they keep me in jail? Will my parents come visit me in jail? Will I be able to go back to school when I get out of jail? Or will I be a convict and not be allowed at school?

What have I done? What am I doing? My hands continue to shake uncontrollably in my lap.

There is some commotion in front of us as the manager confers with his employees. Then they begin to remove the unoccupied stools from the lunch counter. I guess they want to keep more of us from coming in and taking a seat.

There are five of us sitting here. We are not saying a word. Just waiting and watching. I glance sideways and see that the others are also looking straight ahead.

That was what we were told to do. Told. Taught. Trained. A lot of work went into planning today.

Be polite.

Dress well.

Speak clearly when asking to be served.

Say "ma'am" and "sir."

Look straight ahead.

Keep your hands in your lap or by your side.

Do not flinch when they call you names.

Do not respond when you are called such filthy things that it takes your breath away.

Do not turn away when they spit in your face.

Do not raise your arms in defense when they hit you.

Do not resist when they arrest you.

The manager is telling everyone that they are closing up for the day. He is ushering the other white patrons and watchers out. We continue to sit silently at the counter. They would rather close the lunch counter and lose money than serve us a hot dog and a coke.

We continue to sit in the dark in silence after they have cleared everyone else out, hung up the closed sign, and turned off the lights.

We are still sitting like statues when, what seems like hours later, the police arrive.

I recognize the younger officers who are talking to the manager. They are the same ones who come to my granddaddy's auto shop to have their cars worked on. They are customers of his. They are now telling us to put our hands behind our backs to be handcuffed.

As we get up to comply, I glance at the big row of windows that look out onto King Street. There is a crowd of people gathering on the sidewalk to watch. It is a sea of white faces.

I know some of them. I recognize them from around town. I thought they were nice people. I thought they thought I was nice. But all that started to change when we started asking to be treated fairly. To be treated like they were treated. Suddenly they were not as pleasant or friendly. Most of them were downright hostile. Of course, there were a few white people who did stand up for us and with us.

Not today, though. The five of us are the only Negroes and the whites who are watching are silent as we are put in handcuffs and put into the police cruiser.

I've lived in St. Augustine for fifteen years—my whole life. In a house with my mama, daddy, and younger brother, Steven. We live in one side of the house. The other side is where my grandma and granddaddy live. The house is in a part of town called Lincolnville.

That is where all the Negroes live. It is a nice part of town and I like living there. I think most do.

The whites live in other areas of St. Augustine. I guess they like it there. That was fine with us and with them. We were always polite to each other when we would be shopping in the stores downtown.

Those stores had no trouble selling us things and taking our money. But we couldn't sit at the lunch counter and eat. If we wanted to order lunch, we had to pick it up out back and take it home to eat. And we couldn't go swimming at the best beaches in St. Augustine. St. Augustine has some beautiful beaches—but those are designated "whites only."

So I guess all this stuff started bothering us and we began to get the courage to ask why. Why were we treated differently?

Our courage grew when we saw things like the Montgomery Bus Boycott success. Our optimism grew when things like *Brown v. Board of Education* were decided. Our resolve grew when we saw marches, protests, and sit-ins happening around the country. And our fear grew when we saw the violence and hatred that many were forced to endure.

This struggle finally made its way into the consciousness of St. Augustine about six months ago when our city was planning for its 400th anniversary.

Yes, our city is the oldest city in the America! A pretty big deal. And as the city started planning for these great celebrations and activities, we—the Negroes of St. Augustine—asked that we be included.

As you can imagine, this did not sit well with some of the town officials. They were put in their place, though, when word came from the White House (yes, from President John F. Kennedy and vice-president Lyndon Johnson!!!!) that all of our celebrations and events must be integrated. No event could be segregated by race.

A victory, right? You would think so.

However, when vice-president Johnson actually visited this past March for a big party at the very fancy Ponce de Léon Hotel, the city managed to keep it segregated. Any Negroes who bought tickets to the event were seated in a small room, away from the party, and there was even a guard to make sure they didn't leave the room. Can you believe it? Hardly an integrated event!

Well, that did it. That got the Negroes in town pretty stirred up, as you can imagine.

That was when the preachers on Sunday started talking more and more about the Reverend Martin Luther King Jr. and his nonviolent approach to fighting for equal rights. That was when the local chapters of the NAACP and SCLC started holding meetings to talk about and teach us about our rights and about how nonviolent protests were to be carried out. It sounds easy— but being nonviolent can be really, really hard. Especially when someone is screaming horrible things at you or spitting in your face or shoving you.

So here we are . . . sitting in the police cruiser because we wanted to be served like everyone else.

Chapter 2

June 27, 1963

I am sitting in the kitchen listening to my parents in the living room. They are fighting. They don't fight very often, so this is a big deal. I can hear their raised voices through the walls.

"I cannot believe that you think this is okay!" yells my mama.

"I'm not saying it's okay—I'm saying I understand what she did and why." Daddy sounds like he is trying to keep his voice down. Probably hoping it would calm Mama down. "And yes—I support what they are doing. And the way they are doing it."

"Did you know she was going to do this?" Her voice is accusatory.

"No, I had no idea until we got the phone call last night. But . . ." He pauses. I can imagine him looking at her. "We had to know this was going to happen. Since the Reverend King's people have been coming to town and visiting our churches, everyone knows we have rights. It is inevitable that our young people become the most passionate. They have their whole lives ahead of them. Lives that they want to live with the freedoms that all Americans deserve."

"But it is so dangerous." Mama's voice is now becoming quieter and calmer. "I don't want our daughter to become another Emmett Till." Now she is crying.

Soon they are talking so quietly I cannot hear them.

Emmett Till is a name we all know. Every Negro. Maybe whites, too; I am not sure. Back in 1955, he was fourteen years old and he was lynched by the Ku Klux Klan in Mississippi for flirting with a white woman. They brutally killed him—and he was younger than me. He would be twenty-two years old today if he had lived.

For the first time I wonder if I will live to be twenty-two years old. In my mind I have expected the meanness, the aggression, the violence. But I never considered that I might die.

My heart starts beating faster. As fast as it beat last night when Daddy came to pick me up at the jail.

After we were arrested and brought to the station, we called our minister like we were told to. He came to the station with the money to bail us out and called our parents for us.

I was so scared of Daddy's reaction.

Daddy is a big man—tall and bulky. He takes up the whole threshold when he comes into a room. And his voice fits his size—deep and thunderous, even when he is talking calmly. He is also very strict and disciplined. That is his way.

Mama, on the other hand, is tall but thin as a rail. Her slim build is deceiving, though, because she is as strong as an ox. Both physically and mentally.

That is why hearing her cry through the wall is a little unnerving. I've seen Mama cry before, but usually it's been something really tragic like when her mama (my grandmother) died two years ago. She doesn't cry easily.

Unlike me. I am a crybaby. Not a whiny, I-want-my-way crybaby. But when things are emotional, I cry. When I read a sad book, I cry. When I see a sad picture show, I cry. When I hear a sad story, I cry.

I've never liked that about myself, but I can't seem to control it. Daddy says it's because I am empathetic. I hate it when I cry in front of my brother because he will always jump on it as an excuse to tease me.

I thought for sure that when Daddy came to pick me up at the police station, he would start yelling at me and I would start to cry. Instead he just kissed the top of my head and hugged me. It was the longest hug I ever remember getting from him and I could hear his heartbeat through his shirt.

My granddaddy was with him. He is my daddy's daddy and it is easy to see where my daddy gets his size. While Daddy never even looked at any of the police officers, my granddaddy went right up to one of the officers and looked him right in the eyes and said, "So what is all this about, Henry?" Apparently he knew the officer.

The police officer started off trying to explain that we were breaking the law, but before he could even get a whole sentence out, my granddaddy's voice exploded. "This is just rubbish and you know it!" And he turned his back on the officer.

At first I wasn't sure how my granddaddy felt about his granddaughter getting arrested. The ride home in the car was silent. But when we got home and Daddy walked ahead of us, my granddaddy put his hand on my shoulder and turned me around.

"Maggie, I am so proud of you. You and your young friends are going to change the world with your courage and conviction." It was already dark outside so I couldn't see very clearly, but I was sure there were tears in his eyes.

When Daddy and I got inside the house, he simply said, "It's been a long day. Why don't you go up to bed and we will talk about this in the morning."

It was late and I had still not had anything to eat so I was hungry, but Daddy's tone left

no room to argue. "Goodnight, Daddy," I said as I climbed the stairs to bed, my stomach hollow with emotion and hunger.

Later, when Mama and Daddy do come into the kitchen, I can tell that Mama has been crying. The signs are all over her face, even though she is not crying now.

"Well, Margaret Jefferson, we need to talk." Her voice is like steel as she sits down across from me. Daddy stays standing and leans against the counter. Mama's eyes are holding mine so strongly, I can't look anywhere but at her. When she calls me by my given name—Margaret—I know I am in trouble.

"If you are determined to be a part of this, we need to set some rules." There is no room for discussion in her tone, so I just nod.

"There will be no secrets. You must let us know what you plan to do, and when, and with whom, and where."

"Okay," I agree.

"No surprises!" she stresses. I nod again.

"Your father has agreed to become more involved himself." Her voice softens just a bit. "He will be going to any meetings with you and will be working with the other adults in both the NAACP and the SCLC. This will allow us to stay totally informed." Her voice drops to almost a whisper. "And to keep you safe."

"Okay," I agree again.

Later that night Daddy decides he is going to attend the St. Augustine City Commission meeting. Henry Twine from the NAACP is scheduled to speak. I go with Daddy.

I've never been to a city commission meeting before. It is packed with people. I don't know if it is always like this, or if the crowds are here because of what has been happening.

Once the meeting is called to order, there is some boring

business taken care of. Eventually, Mr. Twine is called to speak.

He wants to know why the city of St. Augustine is still segregated, when the commission is telling the outside world that we are an integrated city.

One of the city officials says that St. Augustine is fully integrated and Mr. Twine explodes.

He says that Negroes have been banned from the public library and the city golf course. He says that the McCrory's and Woolworth's lunch counters are still closed because of yesterday's sit-ins.

My cheeks start to burn and Daddy reaches out to hold my hand.

At this point there is a lot of shouting from both the city commissioners and Mr. Twine. Then some of the people attending the meeting start to shout—both Negroes and whites are shouting. It gets to the point where no one can even keep track of who is saying what.

I wonder if things will ever be peaceful again.

Chapter 3

July 18, 1963

My second arrest has happened today. It has been three weeks since the first time I felt the steel of the handcuffs on my wrists, and I thought maybe this time would be easier and less scary. It wasn't.

These weeks have been filled with protests and sit-ins around the city.

At the city commission meeting Daddy and I went to, the commissioners kept saying that St. Augustine was integrated already. I knew that was a lie. Then the commissioners passed more laws limiting the size of the signs that can be used in pickets, and limiting where and when protests could take place. I bet they wanted to outlaw protests altogether but they knew that they would never get away with that.

Our right to protest is protected in the Bill of Rights. "The right to peaceably assemble." I know that from my history classes at school, but I know that everybody knows that now because of the meetings we've been having at church to let everyone know.

So when the city commission tried to limit protests, that just seemed to make it worse, like throwing lighter fluid on a smoldering twig to put out the fire. It will just burst into flames.

So these three weeks have been filled with protests and sit-ins.

Every day there is a group somewhere. The organizers say that this will "keep the issue alive" and will show our resolve.

It also seems to be making some whites madder and madder. Maybe because now our town is in the national news—and not in a good way. All the big news stations have sent reporters here. They are taking pictures and writing articles. There was even a big deal made about the money that was given to St. Augustine for our 400th anniversary celebration we had last winter. I heard someone say that the city might have to give the money back to the federal government. No wonder those white city commissioners are mad.

I have been involved in some of the protests that have been going on. I marched with a group in front of the library. I picketed a laundry that had a "Whites Only" sign. I was even with a group that sang hymns in front of a church that does not allow Negroes to attend their Sunday services. Can you imagine that? I'm pretty sure God does not care what color your skin is if you want to come worship at His church.

Today I was part of another sit-in at a lunch counter. Actually, several sit-ins at several lunch counters around town. The organizers had us work in teams of four, and we all headed out to different places.

Looking around the holding cell where they have put us all, I count sixteen of us. I think my friend Cynthia and I are the youngest. I am guessing the oldest ones here are about twenty years old.

We are all pretty quiet, although I am amazed at how calm and relaxed some of them look. Me? My stomach is doing somersaults. Maybe it is a good thing we did not get served, because if there was any food in my stomach, I was pretty sure I would be throwing it up.

For some reason, this arrest is not like the first one. That time, the officers let us call someone, then they gave us all a talk about how this kind of thing has to stop, how it helps no one, and how we need to remember to obey the law. Then we were picked up.

This time is different. No phone calls. No visitors. No lecture from the officers. We are all just left in the cell as the hours go by. I don't know how much time goes by, but I know it is a lot.

Eventually a couple of officers come and tell us that that they will be separating the girls and the boys and putting us in new cells where we will spend the night. This terrifies me!

Luckily they do put Cynthia and me in the same cell. It is a rectangle room, with stone walls and two cots in it.

Trying to sleep is impossible, even though I am exhausted. Even with my clothes on, the rough sheet and blanket make me itchy. The pillow is like a rock.

Cynthia rolls on her side to face me.

"How long do you think we will be here?" she asks.

"I have no idea," I say calmly, although inside I am a mess. I wonder if I have the courage to do what I know needs to be done.

Nothing will ever change until someone has the conviction to say that it must change. And the courage to do what it takes to force change.

That is what my grandmother told me last week as we sat on the porch swing together. The sun was setting so the heat of the summer day was fading. After we had washed the dinner dishes, we decided to sit outside a bit. It was just the two of us. I had asked her if she thought I was doing the right thing by getting involved in the movement here in St. Augustine.

Then she reached over and took my hand. I think that was her way of saying how proud she was of me.

Lying here tonight, in this cell, I am wondering if I do have the courage to do what it takes to force change.

Chapter 4

July 20, 1963

Home. I don't know if I have ever been so happy to arrive home as I was getting home today.

Our minister, Mr. Eubanks, and Dr. Hayling were doing everything they could to get the sixteen of us released from jail. Justice may be blind, but it is also slow.

It took almost two days before they brought Cynthia and me before a judge. The courtroom was not filled with people. There was not a jury. It did not look like the courtrooms look on TV. There were no lawyers arguing or presenting evidence.

The sheriff just told the judge what we had done and that we had broken the law.

The judge didn't say much at first. Even with judge's bench in front of him, I could tell he was a big man, and the warmth of a Florida July was causing him to sweat. He kept wiping his face with a handkerchief he had in his hand. He let the sheriff finish talking and then looked at us over the top of his eyeglasses.

He furrowed his brow and scowled at us before taking a deep breath.

He started out by saying that we looked like nice young ladies, then his tone quickly turned nasty as he told us how terrible it was that we were disrupting life for others. He went on and on about how the good citizens and the good business owners of St. Augustine deserved better than having people who had no business being there coming in and showing such disrespect for the rules.

I still wasn't sure how Negroes asking to be served at the same lunch counter as the whites was disrespectful, but of course, I didn't say anything and neither did Cynthia.

After the judge had said over and over, in as many different ways as he could, that Cynthia and I were disrespectful and criminals for breaking the law, he started in on what he thought he should do with us.

He explained that any good judge would have to follow the law and lock us up indefinitely.

This scared me more than anything else had ever scared me in my life. I imagined living the rest of my life in the cell where I spent the last two days, with its gray stone walls, little cot with the brown itchy blanket, and the pillow like a rock.

Then he stopped talking, pulled off his glasses, and set to cleaning the lenses while he let us ponder what he had just said.

Then he put his glasses back on, took a deep breath, and told us again that we seemed like nice girls.

"Tell you what," he said. "If you promise that you will not participate in any more sit-ins, I will let you go home."

I don't know who agreed first, or even how long it took us to say the words, but both Cynthia and I agreed to his terms.

Sitting here on my bed after two days in jail, I should feel relieved. But I don't. I feel terrible. Of the fourteen of us arrested, ten of us have been let go because we agreed to the judge's terms. But four would not. They are still in jail.

Chapter 5

July 24, 1963

The July sun is something fierce. In no time at all I can feel my skin heating up, and not soon after that, I am perspiring through my cotton dress. But that doesn't stop me. It doesn't stop any of us.

There are so many people here in front of the St. Johns County jail, that you can barely breathe. There has to be nearly a hundred of us. All ages. Some old, some young, some in between. Men and women. And we are all Negroes. I do not see a white face among us.

We are picketing. We are protesting the fact that Judge Charles Mathis has refused to free the "St. Augustine Four." That is what they are being called now. Audrey Nell Edwards, JoeAnn Anderson, Willie Carl Singleton, and Samuel White.

They were part of the group of sixteen of us arrested almost a week ago. They are not agreeing to the judge's terms like the rest of us did.

When we got word of this protest, Daddy said he was going to be part of it.

"Me too," I said.

When Mama looked at me, I was quick to defend myself.

"I promised the judge I wouldn't participate in any more sit-ins. I didn't say anything about pickets." I looked over at Daddy. He had his head down, but I could see a smile tugging at the sides of his mouth. I knew then he would be on my side.

I felt such a need to come and be a part of this protest. I think mainly because, deep down inside, I am feeling like a sellout.

I don't know how those four found the courage to refuse the judge. They were certainly not intimidated like I was. I wonder what they had, deep down inside, that I did not.

Yes, they are all older than me. But only by five or so years. I wonder if that makes a difference. I wonder if, in five years, I will have the courage to do what they did.

I wonder if this struggle will still be going on in five years.

I wonder if I will still have this heavy feeling inside of me every time I think of this. This feeling of failing.

There are many police watching us from across the street. The protest is very peaceful, but because there are so many of us, I guess it looks aggressive. Some are carrying signs, some are chanting.

We are walking . . . and walking . . . and walking . . . and walking. Up and down the sidewalk in front of the county jail.

We are not stopping traffic, so cars are passing us and I can see them slowing down. Their mostly white faces looking at us, or reading the signs maybe. They don't seem to be horrified by what has happened to four Negro youths, or bothered by the fact that one hundred or more of us are protesting. They only seem curious about what the ruckus is all about.

Chapter 6

July 26, 1963

I am helping Mama snap the beans for tonight's dinner, when Daddy walks into the kitchen and slams the newspaper on the table.

"The story is all over the news. The *Daytona Beach Morning Journal* has an editorial in there today that tells the world what Judge Mathis is doing and it does not look kindly on his approach." Daddy sits down at the table and goes on.

"They come right out and say that what he is doing—keeping those four kids in jail—is just plain wrong. They even quote someone from the U.S. Commission on Civil Rights who says that he has no right asking those young people to promise not to picket or protest as a condition of their release." He pauses again. "And this is even a white paper printing this," he adds, as if that makes it hold more weight.

Which I guess it does. If a Negro paper had printed an article saying what Judge Mathis was doing was wrong, no one would pay attention. But when a white paper says something, it means something.

"Do you think this will make a difference?" Mama asks as she dries her hands on her apron, sits down at the table, and pulls the paper in front of her to have a look.

"We can hope," he says.

By the time Mama finishes reading the newspaper, it's time to set the table for dinner. That means I am helping in the kitchen for the next couple hours. Helping Mama cook, serve, and do the dishes and clean up.

By the time I get the chance to read the article, it is getting late, and since no one else in the family seems interested, I take the newspaper to my room.

Sitting on my bed, I read the article. Then I read it again.

When I read about the sixteen people arrested, my cheeks turn red even though no one is in my room. I know I am one of the sixteen the writer is referring to when he says "these courageous young people."

I am not feeling courageous. Especially when I read about the twelve who agreed to Judge Mathis's conditions. I am one of the twelve. Once again I get a hollow feeling inside of me. He doesn't name the twelve, but he does name the "St. Augustine Four"—the ones still being held—Audrey, JoeAnn, Willie, and Samuel.

The writer says that we should all—ALL AMERICANS—be horrified that this can happen in our country.

Powerful words.

But are words enough?

Chapter 7

August 28, 1963

We are all gathered in the living room. Me, my brother, Mama, Daddy, Granddaddy, and Grandma. We are watching the TV news report on the March on Washington being led by Dr. Martin Luther King Jr.

Our TV is small, so we are all sitting close and Daddy turned the volume up pretty loud.

I have never been to Washington, DC, although I have certainly studied about it in my history classes. Of course I recognize the Lincoln Memorial and the Reflecting Pool where the spectators have gathered at the end point of the march.

The news reporters are talking about the size of the crowds and how they are peacefully marching to raise awareness of the fact that Negroes in this country are not treated equally.

I wonder—are there really people in our country who are not aware of how unfairly the Negroes are treated? Are there really people who believe segregation is a fair and good thing?

Well, there must be, or the protests and this Civil Rights Movement would not be met with such violence, I suppose.

The reporters are also talking about all of the speakers who have spoken today and what they have all said. They pause to tell us that Dr. King will speak next. That is what we are waiting for.

My mama and daddy are great believers in Dr. King. They followed his work with the people of Montgomery when they fought to get the busses integrated. They wept when his home was bombed. They read so many of his speeches and writings.

When Dr. King begins to speak, Daddy turns the volume up even louder and we listen.

I love the way he talks. I can tell that my little brother doesn't understand many of the words Dr. King is using, and probably doesn't understand the points he is making, but I do.

I listen to his words and they fill my head with visions of how things are supposed to be. I listen to his ideas and my heart fills with wishing and hoping and believing.

I have a dream that my four little children will one day live in a nation where they will not be judged by the color of their skin but by the content of their character. I have a dream today. . . .

I look over and tears are running down my grandma's face. I can't see Mama's face, but I can see her wiping her cheeks. That makes me not feel badly about the tears that are overflowing from my eyes.

Later that night as I lay in bed in the dark, I can still hear the echo of Dr. King's words in my head.

So let freedom ring . . . when this happens and we allow freedom to ring . . . we will be able to join hands and sing . . . "Free at Last" . . .

And I wonder if the world he talks about is even possible. A world where it won't matter what the color of your skin is, because everyone will be treated equally.

I think it must be possible, because today was an important day.

Not only in Washington, but here in St. Augustine, Florida, too.

Today, two of our neighbors enrolled their children at Fullerwood Elementary. The all-white school.

Chapter 8

September 2, 1963

For the first time, we are holding our demonstration at the *Plaza de la Constitución*. The St. Augustine Town Plaza. The center of the historic district. It is a green grassy area surrounded by streets that wrap its perimeter. The Bridge of Lions is across the street at the east side and the Old Government House building is at the west end.

This is the heart of Old St. Augustine, where tourists come. When families want to visit the oldest, continuously inhabited European settlement In the United States, they come here. When people want to visit the Castillo de San Marcos—the coquina fort—they come here. When people want to visit the fancy hotels of Henry Flagler, these are the streets they walk.

I am sure that is why the organizers picked this spot. So that anyone visiting St. Augustine will realize that it is still a deeply segregated place. I am also sure that is why there are so many police officers here as well.

We—the protesters—are walking in a long line around the outside edge of the plaza with our signs. Signs that say segregation is unacceptable. We are a big group of all ages. Daddy is here with me, but this time my granddaddy came, too. Daddy is in front of me and my granddaddy behind me.

The tourists and visitors to the city are definitely interested in what is going on. They stop. They watch. They talk. It is hard to tell if they are supporting us or if they are against us.

It is easy to tell that the police are against us. Another group of officers arrive and they begin to gather together. It seems they are getting instructions.

They approach the marchers and demand that we stop. We do not even acknowledge their presence and keep marching. Before I know it, I begin to hear yells and screams. The officers are rushing the line of peaceful marchers with cattle prods. These are long metal rods used to shock cattle into moving. They are hard, sharp, and some are electrified.

Everything seems to be happening in slow motion in my mind. As the dozens of officers begin to storm us, the orderly, straight line of protesters breaks apart. Some begin to run to try to avoid the sharp rods. I see people fall to the ground. I hears screams and cries.

From my right I see an officer rushing my daddy, the metal prod aimed straight out at him. He does not notice because he is helping up a woman in front of him who fell. I can hear the crack as the metal prod hits his back and then I hear a crackle. As he falls to the ground, I scream.

The officer turns and aims the prod at me. I am so stunned, I freeze. As the officer leans toward me, my granddaddy jumps in front of me and his arm gets hit with the prod. He loses his balance and falls as well.

By the time I help my granddaddy and my daddy up, the officer is gone. He has moved on to inflict his shock on others.

Amidst the chaos that has now taken over the Plaza de la Constitución, the three of us stumble home.

Chapter 9

September 15, 1963

Sitting in stunned silence, my family is once again gathered in the living room, our eyes glued to the images on the television screen.

This time it is not inspiring, like the marches we watched three weeks ago. This time it is not hopeful, like the speeches we listened to that day. This time does not bring tears of joy.

My mama, who rarely cries, is sitting forward in her chair, her hand over her mouth, and tears stream down her face. My grandma is sitting ramrod straight on the sofa, my granddaddy next to her. They are holding hands. His left hand and arm are still bandaged from the cattle prod. Daddy is once again standing behind the sofa, his hands gripping the cushions as he stares at the screen.

The 16th Street Baptist Church in Birmingham, Alabama, was bombed today. The television shows the smoldering rubble behind the news reporter, as he informs us that the Ku Klux Klan has taken responsibility for the bombing.

I am listening to his words, but I am staring at the church behind him. It looks similar to our church. At least what is left of it seems to. The same kind of brick. The same crosses. The bomb went off this morning during Sunday services.

Four girls were killed. They were all between eleven and fourteen years old. Younger than me.

The world is going crazy.

Because we—the Negroes of this country—are demanding that we be treated fairly, we have turned ourselves into targets.

Chapter 10

September 19, 1963

As I walk into the kitchen, Mama and Daddy are sitting at the kitchen table talking quietly. They stop when I come in and look up. Mama's face is tear stained.

I don't know what to say. This mama who has been crying so much lately is not the mama I'm used to.

I sit down at the table and just wait for them to say something. I know they have news.

"Dr. Hayling and three other men were kidnapped by the local Ku Klux Klan yesterday and beaten nearly to death."

The silence hangs heavy in the air. I know Daddy doesn't expect me to say anything, but the moment feels like it needs a comment.

"What?" My voice is almost a whisper.

"Dr. Hayling, Mr. Hauser, Mr. Jackson, and Mr. Jenkins were taken at gunpoint yesterday. They were taken to a Klan gathering outside of town and beaten with sticks and rocks and pipes."

I don't know the other three names, but I know Dr. Hayling. He is our dentist. He came to St. Augustine a number of years ago and opened his dental office. Not only do the colored folks go to him, but a good number of whites do, too.

He is a nice man. Funny. Friendly.

I can't imagine someone would hate anyone enough to beat them with pipes and bricks.

I am still sitting stunned when Grandma and Granddaddy come in. Apparently they have already heard the news.

"They are all in the hospital," Granddaddy says. "There is a police officer keeping watch on their rooms."

"Thank goodness!" Mama gushes. "Those Klan people could come and try to finish the job."

"The police aren't there to protect them," Granddaddy says. "They are there because they are the ones being charged with trespassing and assault."

"What?" I say again.

It seems inconceivable. How could they charge them when they were the ones kidnapped at gunpoint and beaten up? My head just cannot wrap itself around this.

All of a sudden, Mama is all business.

"The Klan is getting bolder and more aggressive. We have to be more careful than ever before." She is looking at me.

"No more going out after dark unless you are with one of us. No more going to town alone, even if you are just running errands in the middle of the day. No more . . . "

The directions Mama is outlining rattle in my head. I am no longer listening.

Chapter 11

October 22, 1963

I am sitting on my bed, reading my assigned pages in my textbook. It is past my usual bedtime, but I am not tired and I can't seem to quiet my mind. I am hoping that by focusing on my homework, I can push other things out of my mind.

I have been a good student for as long as I have been a student. Mama and Daddy always made clear that education is important. Not something to be taken lightly or taken for granted.

That was not a problem for me. I have always loved learning, and school just seems like a good fit for me. I like the teachers. I like the structure. I like the organization of it all.

As I get to the end of the page—again—and realize I don't know what I read—again—I sigh and close the book.

I lean back against the pillow on my bed, and that is when I hear it. Actually, I feel it too.

An explosion. The whole house seems to rattle and I can practically feel the vibration pulse through my body.

The silence that follows seems eternal as I wait for something else to happen—the roof to collapse . . . the house to burst into flames . . . screams to fill the air.

But the silence continues. Then I hear Mama and Daddy at the foot of the stairs, opening the front door to the porch.

I jump up and I am right behind them as they step out onto the porch, but Mama pushes me back inside.

"You stay put." Her voice is like steel so I stay where I am. With the door open, though, I can look down the street.

That's when I see the flames shooting out of the window of the Brunson family's home. They live five houses down on the other side of the street.

Daddy, Granddaddy, and several others rush down the street. I hear the yelling and I see the panic, but it still does not seem real.

The next several hours are a blur. The neighbors put the fire out before the fire engine even arrives. From the outside of the house, I can see the scorch marks and the ash near the broken window where the firebomb was thrown into their home. But other than that, the house does not look too badly damaged.

No one was hurt. All three of the kids—fourth grader Irvin, Billy in sixth grade, and Debbie in second grade—were in the back of the house with both Mr.and Mrs. Brunson. While they seem upset, Mr. and Mrs. Brunson do not seem shocked. How is it that we have reached a place where a firebomb thrown at your house does not shock you?

They are such a nice family. I wonder why it was their house. Then I remember.

Billy, Irvin, and Debbie are now going to the white school.

Chapter 12

November 21, 1963

I am once again sitting on my bed, flipping through the latest issue of *JET* Magazine.

It has been almost a month since the Brunson's house was firebombed. We later found out that all of the families whose children are going to the white school had firebombs thrown at their houses that night.

Although no one was hurt in the attacks, it seems to give the hateful whites who are angry about the thought of desegregation the courage to continue to make trips into our neighborhoods to try to intimidate us.

Seems every night, somewhere in Lincolnville, you will see some big car driving slowly down our streets, three or four white men in the car. They always wait till the sun goes down and they always make sure that if we are looking, we see their shotguns leaning on their shoulders or sitting on the seats beside them. Even in the dark we can see the ominous reflection of the moon or the streetlight off the metal.

Sometimes someone will have on a Klan hood, but most times it seems they don't care that we see who they are.

One of the men in one of those cars was shot and died.

A week or so later they arrested five Negro men and charged them. They say there is no real evidence that they did it, but I guess that does not matter. It was the same judge who freed the whites charged with kidnapping and beating Dr. Hayling.

I flip past the articles on makeup and clothes and get to the article, *Oldest City in the US Most Backward in Race Relations.*

I don't know if this article should make me feel better or make me feel worse.

Better because it means what we have been saying and experiencing here in St. Augustine is not going on everywhere. That there are parts of our country where Negroes are treated better.

Or should I feel worse because this is my town. My home. And the world now knows our shortcomings.

Or maybe I should feel hopeful because, with the attention these kinds of articles focus on St. Augustine, the town will maybe be more likely to change.

Chapter 13

November 28, 1963

Today is Thanksgiving. This is always one of my most favorite holidays. That is because the only things you have to think about are being with your family to share a meal and being thankful for your blessings.

No presents. No costumes. No hiding colored eggs. No fireworks. I like its simplicity.

I also love the fact that it centers around the table. I make extra sure that everything looks nice as I set the table for dinner. The table is extra large right now. Daddy laid a big piece of plywood over the top of our table and then we spread a big gold-colored tablecloth over it. Now the table will be big enough to fit all of those who will be with us this year.

There will be sixteen of us. Mama has been cooking since early morning. Mama loves Thanksgiving even more than I do, I think. She loves to have lots of people to cook for.

Usually, when she was preparing for a meal like this, she would be downright cheerful as she cooks and bakes.

Not today. Not this year. It is hard to be cheerful when things seem so unfair. When violence seems to be part of the fabric of everyday life. It was just six days ago when I heard the words. . . .

"The president's been shot."

I was sitting in history class with my book open to World War I. We were reviewing for an upcoming exam.

Mrs. Williams, sitting at her desk in the front of the room with her book open, looked at the assistant principal, the one who launched those words into our classroom from the doorway.

No one moved. The words were simple, yet they made no sense. John F. Kennedy? Our young, handsome president with the pretty wife and small children? He was shot?

Within minutes we were gathered around a radio, listening to the reports.

The president had been shot.

Then we heard that he had died.

By the time I got home from school that afternoon, it felt like the whole world had changed.

By the time everyone arrives and Thanksgiving dinner is on the table, I feel better. I sense that Mama does, too. As we take our seats around the table, this feels right. It feels good. It feels safe.

My younger cousin and my brother rush to get the same seat. My brother wins with a grin on his face. My uncle is raving about the spread on the table, while my aunt is adjusting dishes in the center so they all fit. Mama cautions everyone to save room for dessert.

We all hold hands and bow our heads as Daddy leads our prayer.

He talks about how, in an uncertain world, we can always count on God and our family. He says that faith has got to be something we care for and nurture, because faith will take us where we need to be. Faith will give us courage to persevere.

Then he talks about the endless blessings that have been bestowed on all of us and how they can never be taken for granted.

And last, he asks for God's guidance as we each do our part to bring about positive change in the world.

My "amen" to his last statement is louder than I intend it to be. I hope He hears this prayer. Guide me as I try to do my part to bring about positive change in the world.

Six months ago I thought I knew what I needed to do. I thought it sounded easy.

Well—maybe not easy, but doable. I thought I could march. Protest. Sit in. Be arrested.

But I never thought beyond that. I thought I had the courage to be part of this movement. Now I am not so sure.

Ever since I promised Judge Mathis I would not participate in anymore sit-ins, I can't shake the feeling that I am a sellout. A coward. I folded, when others had not.

Chapter 14

January 15, 1964

Pulling open the front door, I sense that something is wrong. I am arriving home from school and I hear Mama and Daddy talking in the kitchen. Daddy is never home from work this early. I wonder what terrible thing has happened now.

A year or so ago, if Daddy had been home when I got home from school, I would have just been curious, wondering why. Maybe even thinking something exciting or good had happened. A surprise.

Now, my first thoughts are that something terrible has happened. Someone's house got bombed. Someone got shot. Someone got kidnapped and beat up. The Ku Klux Klan did something to someone. Or even the police.

I silently scold myself for being so negative. But I think that in this last year, the world has changed. Or maybe just my world has changed. Or maybe I am now just living in this harsh world, no longer wrapped up in the cocoon of my protected childhood.

I put my books on the table and walk into the kitchen. Daddy looks up from the newspaper and I see he is grinning.

"Have a seat, Maggie!" he says almost joyfully.

As I sit across from him, he tells me that the Florida state legislature yesterday ordered the release of the "St. Augustine Four."

It seems the scathing national publicity that our state has been receiving because four teenagers have been in jail for over five months because of a sit-in, has been more than the legislature can take.

They want this negative publicity to go away. They want the rest of the country to once again hear "Florida" and think sunshine and beaches and vacations. Not sit-ins, the Ku Klux Klan, protests, and four teenagers in jail—just for trying to be served a hamburger and a milkshake.

I wonder if this will work. I wonder if letting them out of jail will stop the protests, the newspaper articles, the attention St. Augustine has been getting.

I also wonder if, now that they will be out of jail, my feelings of guilt and failure will go away.

I realize I am looking at my hands and look up. Daddy is staring at me.

"It's over, baby—you do not have to feel like you let down the movement. You did just what you were supposed to do."

Tears fill my eyes. How did he know the burden I have been carrying?

Chapter 15

February 8, 1964

Daddy was wrong. It is not over. All the hope that I felt three weeks ago has been slowly evaporating like a puddle of water in the sun.

The Florida legislature ordering the release of LeeAnn, Audrey, Willie, and Samuel has not changed a thing.

I am sitting at the kitchen table with my brother, helping him do his homework. He is doing subtraction where he has to borrow and regroup numbers. He is having a really hard time with it. I check the first list of problems and they are all wrong. I erase his answers and his shoulders droop

"It's okay. We can do a couple together for practice," I tell him. I take him through the steps again.

I am babysitting my brother because Mama and Daddy are out. They are at a meeting at church—which is kind of unusual for a Saturday. Although maybe not unusual given the events of the last couple of weeks. Especially the last two days. The last twenty-four hours.

It was less than three weeks ago that Mr. Brunson's car was bombed. It was not sitting here in his driveway on our street. It was parked at Fullerwood Elementary School. Mr. and Mrs. Brunson were inside attending the school PTA Meeting. That must have been some meeting.

I try to imagine the courage it takes to walk into a room full of white folks, being just about the only Negro there. Knowing that they do not want you there.

The car bomb did not hurt anyone, but it totally destroyed their car. I wonder how they will get around now.

Then yesterday the Robersons' house, three blocks over, was firebombed. Their son is also enrolled at Fullerwood. But unlike when the Brunsons' house was bombed and the fire was put out quick, this firebomb destroyed the entire house.

As if that was not enough, Dr. Hayling's house was also shot up. Someone—or two or three people—drove by and sprayed his house full of bullets. Broke windows, went through walls, and ended up killing his dog. His dog!

I remember him talking about his dog to me when I had a dentist appointment once. I think he liked talking about his dog to the kids he saw because it got our minds off the reason we were there. I remember him saying that his dog loved to have his belly rubbed and loved eating raw green beans. That made me laugh, thinking about a dog eating green beans.

Thinking about the dog and Dr. Hayling now, I have such a feeling of sadness. I am also feeling sad for the Brunsons and the Robersons.

I reach over and pull my brother into a hug. I am also feeling sad for us. Sad that this is now our life. Sad that people we know are losing their cars and their houses and their dogs to violence.

I know, and believe, that Dr. King is right. We have to force change using nonviolence. But I wonder how long people can have violence thrust upon them and continue to turn the other cheek.

Chapter 16

March 20, 1964

The room is packed, and I mean packed, with people. We are in the church and the pews are full, people taking up less space than normal just so another person can fit. The aisles are also full as people who can't find seats, stand. It is never this full on Sunday, when the preacher is giving his sermons and we are all gathered to pray and worship. I wonder if that bothers him.

We are here to get information and get organized for the protests of the next week or so. The eyes of the country continue to stay focused on St. Augustine. The city officials say this is a great place and that we have no racial issues and that it is only a few troublemakers.

Yet they also admit that St. Augustine has segregation laws. And those laws will be followed. How that is "no racial issues," I have no idea.

The Southern Christian Leadership Conference, Dr. King's organization, has even started to take notice of St. Augustine. Some of our local leaders from the NAACP, with Dr. Hayling and Mr. Eubanks, even drove to Orlando a couple weeks ago to talk with Dr. King and others who might help.

That is what this day is about. We want to find out what went on and what the plan is and what we should each do.

I am sitting next to Cynthia. Neither of us has been to any sit-ins since our arrest last July. We have attended protests and other gatherings, but have not sat down at a segregated lunch counter and asked to be served. It may sound silly, but I think it is important that we have kept our word to that judge. Daddy says a man's word is his bond.

Next to Cynthia and me are so many of our friends from school. I do not think there are too many people at my school who are NOT involved in "the movement."

That's what we call it—the movement. I like the way it sounds. It sounds like progress. It sounds like change. It sounds peaceful.

As we sit here, we first hear about how supportive the SCLC and the NAACP are of what we are doing in St. Augustine. We are also told that in just a few days, "Supporters from the north" will be arriving in St. Augustine to stand with us in protest. Students, teachers, clergy—mostly white, from universities in the north—are coming to St. Augustine to be part of our demonstrations.

The plan is to have small groups, including both whites and colored folks, go into businesses, churches, parks, libraries, and other public places together, which would be a violation of the segregation laws. The obvious goal: to be arrested for breaking these laws. The hope is that the arrests will make the news reports all over, not just in Florida.

The more people know about the unjustness of these laws, the sooner they will change. That is the hope.

We spend the next hour or so getting specific information—who will be our group organizer, what businesses we might go to, when and where to meet again to share information.

Chapter 17

March 31, 1964

The sun is warm for March, but the breeze off the bay is keeping us from getting too warm. I am dressed in my Sunday pink wool skirt and white blouse. It is one of the nicest outfits I own.

We are marching in rows of three or four and our line goes on forever! There are nearly a hundred and fifty of us and we are all students from my high school—Murray High School. We are singing hymns and freedom songs. Some have linked arms.

The songs are soulful and hopeful. Songs of freedom and liberty.

We are all dressed in our best outfits. That is because our destination is the Ponce de León Hotel.

It has been a busy couple of weeks. As predicted, more than thirty teachers and students from northern colleges arrived to participate in our demonstrations. Even the mother of the Massachusetts governor is here! Yes, her son—her white son—is the governor of a state and she came down to protest with us.

She even managed to get herself arrested! She is being charged with breaking the segregation laws. I was there yesterday as the police put her in the back seat of the police cruiser to take her off to jail and she was actually smiling! She was happy to be sitting in handcuffs.

That made me smile. She looked like someone's little gray-haired grandmother, sitting in the back seat of a squad car in her Easter coat and hat. Hands in handcuffs and a smile on her face.

As the Ponce de Léon Hotel comes into view, I suck in my breath. It is so beautiful. Built by Henry Flagler in the 1880s, it quickly became one of the fanciest hotels of its time. While it might not be one of the fanciest now after all these years, it has always been on the list of what sets St. Augustine apart.

And it is clearly a place where colored people are not welcome—unless of course, you work there, washing floors or windows or serving guests.

That is what we are protesting today.

As we climb the front steps of the grand hotel, I can see the employees and guests watching, not sure what we are going to do.

Our march continues up the steps, through the entryway with the soaring ceiling, and up another set of steps into the dining room of the exclusive hotel.

As we march into the massive circular room, I cannot take my eyes off the stained glass windows. Tiffany glass. The colors are breathtaking.

We begin to fill up the tables, pulling the substantial chairs out and taking all the available seats around the room.

The tables are all set beautifully. The linen tablecloths are snow white and hang almost to the floor. Each table has small vases and candles in the center and the tables are set with china and crystal. Although we were not told to, most of us put our hands in our laps. I am sure they are thinking what I am—I do not want to break any of these stunning dishes or glassware. I have never seen anything so beautiful, as the light from the window dances across the room to reflect and refract from and through the glasses.

It does not take long for a large group of the sheriff's men to come strutting into the room.

One of them has a bullhorn and proceeds to tell us that we are breaking the law and will be treated accordingly. We are to immediately vacate the dining room and file right back out the door we came in. If we do that, we will not be arrested, he tells us. As if that is a generous gift he is bestowing on us and we should all be grateful.

I glance around without turning my head. No one is moving. He waits a few seconds and repeats his speech.

Again, nothing happens. I can tell he is getting frustrated.

He begins again, this time telling us that if we do not do as he says, he cannot guarantee that we will not be hurt, as his officers will have to use force to remove us.

That is when my breathing becomes shallow and my heart begins racing. I see some of the men in uniform taking out cattle prods. I remember the sight and sound and smell from the first time I saw these tools used on my daddy and granddaddy. It will be me this time who yells in pain and wears the scars.

Chapter 18

April 1, 1964

I am sitting on the couch. It is after dinner and it feels terribly wrong to be sitting here while Mama is in the kitchen cleaning up and doing the dishes. These things are usually my chores. But the bandages on my arms make it nearly impossible. Mama did not seem to mind. But I do.

Actually, Mama was smiling as she hugged me and said to go sit and read while she finished up.

The bandages go from my wrist to nearly my shoulder on my left arm. That was the side the police officer came from as I was sitting quietly at the table in the Ponce de Léon dining room. At first I didn't see him—I felt him. Well, I felt the cattle prod. It tore into my arm with a shock and fire.

My right arm is bandaged, too, but only between my wrist and elbow. That is not a cattle prod injury. That was when I fell as I tried to get up and get away from that officer. I tripped and fell onto the floor, landing right on a goblet that had fallen onto the floor and shattered. That injury, while less painful than the burns from the cattle prod, had bled something fierce.

Grandma comes in and sits in her favorite chair.

"Nice break from doing the dishes?" she asks. "Or are you feeling badly about not helping?"

How does she always know how I am feeling? I shrug as she comes to sit next to me.

"How are the arms feeling?" she asks as she takes my right hand into hers. Her hands are small and her skin feels soft, but I know these hands are strong hands. Strong like her, in spite of her small stature. I wonder how I can have such strong women in my family—her on my daddy's side, and my mama—and yet not be strong myself. How can that be?

"They're okay," I tell her. I hate that my voice sounds whiny.

"You young people did good yesterday. That was a very brave thing you all did." She squeezes my hand.

I look down into my lap. While my hand is bigger than hers, feeling the warmth of hers makes me feel safe. I shrug my shoulders again. I certainly am not feeling brave.

"Did you know that this week's protests and arrests are all over the news? The national news?" Grandma says to me as she picks up a copy of the newspaper from the table and hands it to me.

"All the country is beginning to realize what is going on here. Like so many places in this country. And they are seeing how brave our people are." Her voice sounds sad and full of pride at the same time.

She stands up, kisses the top of my head, and leaves the room.

I open the newspaper and scan the front page. It has a picture of Mrs. Peabody, the mother of that governor, after her arrest. She is sitting in the back of a police car with her hands handcuffed. She is looking out the window and she is smiling in her coat and hat. Not a forced smile, but nearly a grin. She is obviously happy that she got arrested.

I read the article. The article not only explains about the northerners coming here to stand with the Negroes in protest, but quotes the mayor of St. Augustine, Joseph Shelley. Boy, is he mad!

He blames the national news and networks for "misquoting and distorting" what he has said. He blames them for contributing to the problems here in town. And then he goes on to criticize Mrs. Peabody. He says terrible things about her being a troublemaker and sticking her nose in where she has no business being.

I look back at the picture. She looks like somebody's grandmother. I think of my grandma. I can imagine them being friends and having coffee together. She doesn't look like a terrible person at all.

Chapter 19

April 14, 1964

Church is packed today. Even more than normal. Which is amazing since normal services are totally full.

St. Augustine has a lot of churches. A lot! Some even say it is the birthplace of Christianity in America because when the Spanish first landed here in 1565, the first thing they did was have a mass to thank God for their safe journey.

Of course, it was a Catholic mass since the Spanish were mainly Catholic.

As St. Augustine grew, churches seemed to just keep springing up. Why, just on St. George Street alone there must be five or six.

Most churches though, do not welcome colored parishioners. Some do not ban them from coming in, but certainly do not welcome them. Others are downright hostile.

Then there are the colored churches. The ones for us, led by those that look like us, and understand what it means to be us. That means that the churches of St. Augustine, like everything else in town, are segregated. You go to a white church if you are white, you go to a colored church if you are black.

Reverend Peters is giving his usual sermon. I am half listening. Then the word catches my attention. Segregation. I sit up a little straighter and pay attention.

He is talking about Bishop Hamilton West, the Episcopalian leader in Florida. He has issued an order that all Episcopalian churches in Florida will open their doors to anyone who wishes to attend services—regardless of the color of their skin. All Episcopalian churches will no longer be segregated.

Someone shouts "Amen!" from the back of the church. A few begin to applaud, as "Hallelujah!" and "Praise the Lord!" join the chorus of clapping.

After the Reverend quiets the congregation, he goes on to explain what this means. He says that just saying it does not make it so, and that the only way to make sure it happens is to test it.

That means some people will need to attend services at the white congregations in town. He says that some of the white ministers are very supportive of this change, but some are not happy. Some will welcome us, some will not. And the congregations are even more splintered and divided over the issue. Like all protests, he says, we need to be prepared for the worst—hate, aggression, even arrests.

In church? This seems so unbelievable to me. Regardless of what people do and say in town, or at work, I always thought that just being in church softened your heart. Sitting in the presence of the crucifix, seeing statues of Mary and paintings of the apostles surrounded in a sort of peaceful kindness, that it just made you want to act more like Jesus.

Would Jesus really care about who was white and who wasn't? I doubt it. I just can't imagine anyone doing something hateful, on purpose, in church. The thought of what we have endured at our protests and sit-ins, inside of a church rather than a diner or on the street, just seems so much worse. Churches are places of love, acceptance, peace, and safety.

My mind comes back to the Reverend's speech as he begins to talk about how we must welcome, with open arms, any whites who decide they would like to worship at our church.

That surprised me. On one level because I do not believe we need to be reminded of that. After all, we have been fighting against being excluded and treated differently because of our skin color. Why would we subject someone else to what we hate? But I am also surprised because I have never imagined that a white would want to go to a church that is not white.

Chapter 20

May 17, 1964

He is coming to St. Augustine. The Reverend Martin Luther King Jr. He is going to be here tomorrow.

I am so excited. The man who is so often on TV, the man who brought me to tears with his *I Have a Dream* speech, the man who makes me believe that we have the power to change things.

He will be here in St. Augustine. I am so excited. I am also nervous. While he is an important leader for our cause, I also know that he is a target. I wonder if anything will happen to him while he is here. The violence here these last months has been hard to understand and accept.

The bombing of people's homes because their children are going to a specific school.

The shooting of someone's house and dog because they speak out.

The kidnapping and beating of people who want to end segregation.

They say that Dr. King will not even be staying in the same place each night that he is here. He will keep moving so those who want to do him harm will not know for sure where he is. It seems like a good plan, although I am still worried something might happen.

Mama and Daddy must feel the same way because they do not want my little brother playing outside today or tomorrow, they said. Or maybe even the next day.

He doesn't understand why. But I do. They must be worried that someone from the Ku Klux Klan will drive down the streets of Lincolnville and shoot at the houses. Like they have done before.

Not in an effort to actually hit someone, but just to let us know that they are here, and they are armed, and that they can shoot up our neighborhood if they want. That is because nothing will happen to them, even if we call the police. Even if the police come.

That is because some members of the Klan are also members of the local police department. At least that is what I hear people say. The sheriff deputized some local Klan in order to help put us in our place. So that they can drive around, boldly showing their faces, their rifles clearly in sight on their laps, just to show us how powerful they are. And how powerless we are.

Dr. King says our power comes from being right.

Being right didn't help me when I sat at the lunch counter and wanted to order something to eat. Being right got me arrested.

Being right didn't help me when I sat in the Ponce de Léon hotel dining room wanting to be served. Being right got me burned with a cattle prod.

Being right didn't help the St. Augustine Four when they exercised their right to peacefully protest. Being right got them locked up for months.

Being right didn't help Mr. Robertson when he legally enrolled his children in an integrated school. Being right got his house burned down.

Being right didn't help Dr. Hayling when he was kidnapped by the Klan and beaten. Being right got his house shot up and his dog killed.

I shake my head and stand up. I have to stop thinking of all these things. Thinking these thoughts only makes my heart hurt and my hands shake. It doesn't make me feel any better.

Instead I try to focus on Dr. King coming. Listening to him makes me believe that we can change things. That we can force change with our protests, our sit-ins, our marches.

I pick up the newspaper that Daddy left on his chair and sit back down to reread the article about Dr. King. It talks about the Civil Rights Movement that is happening not just here in St. Augustine, but across the country. The article even quotes Dr. King as saying that St. Augustine is a "small Birmingham."

Birmingham, Alabama. The place where the National Guard had to escort young black children as they went to school because their town and state was trying to ban them from attending a school that they had a legal right to attend.

Birmingham, where four young black girls died when their church was bombed.

The article also states that Dr. King is proud and honored to be fighting alongside so many young people who have taken up the cause and are participating in marches, sit-ins, and protests. He says he is strengthened by their courage and conviction.

I know I am one of the "young people" to which he refers. I was arrested. Spit on. Shouted at. Burned with a cattle prod.

But I am not the young person of courage and conviction that he talks about.

I am not courageous. I am petrified.

I am not brave. I am scared.

Chapter 21

May 31, 1964

We are on our way to the Memorial Day gathering at church.

It is always a full celebration. Big tables are set up along the back of the church and everyone brings food. Lots and lots of food. Sometimes I am amazed the tables don't collapse under the weight of all the plates and platters and bowls of food that are stacked on top. Potato salad, corn, meat platters, breads, jams and jellies, fruits, bowls overflowing with vegetables. The tables seem to stretch on forever.

On the grass behind the church are all the temporary tables and folding chairs that everyone has brought. The tables all have tablecloths covering them and a tiny American flag stands in the center of each table.

There is a huge crowd of people. There will be lots of eating, singing, laughter, talking, and visiting. And, of course, honoring those who gave their lives for our country.

Memorial Day is important to our family and our community. That is because there are many families who have lost a loved one.

We always think of Uncle Walter on Memorial Day. Well—we think of him other times, too, but he is first in our thoughts on Memorial Day.

He was Daddy's older brother and he died fighting in World War II. I never knew him, but I have heard the stories.

Daddy used to follow Walter around like a puppy. He helped teach Daddy how to fix engines and rebuild cars. He also taught Daddy how to play football, but Daddy never took to it like Uncle Walter did. He was a high school player and, they say, really good.

Daddy was just sixteen when Uncle Walter enlisted and went off to train to be a soldier. Then he was shipped over to Europe to fight.

It was hard for them all when he died. But they said he was doing his duty for the country that he loved so much.

I wonder what he would think if he was here and saw the trouble going on in the country today. The trouble in St. Augustine. I think that if he was here, and went into the diner with me, or protested, he would have also been arrested, or beaten, or jabbed with a cattle prod.

How can that be? That a soldier who served this country would not be able to sit at a lunch counter and order a sandwich? Just because he was not white. That is disgraceful. Who could think that was okay?

I grab my plate and sit at the table. I hear talking about the shooting at the safe house where Dr. King was last week. Luckily he was not here at the time, but it is obvious that his two visits in a month's time have done nothing to calm things down. In fact, they may have just made things worse, if that is possible.

Chapter 22

June 9, 1964

I cannot believe that Mama and Daddy said yes! Judge Simpson has ruled that St. Augustine cannot legally ban nighttime demonstrations, so a big one is being planned for tonight. Right in downtown St. Augustine, at the town plaza—the old "slave market."

Both Mama and Daddy are with me. My grandparents are home with my little brother.

As we walk the several blocks from Lincolnville to King Street, there are more and more people on the streets the closer we get to downtown.

I am surprised by the crowds. This has got to be the biggest protest I have been a part of. Maybe the biggest I have ever seen. Well . . . not as big as the one Dr. King led in Washington, DC, or as big as the one I saw on TV once in Alabama.

But certainly this is the biggest that has taken place in St. Augustine. My heart starts beating faster. I am excited to see so many people.

It is a sea of bodies and faces and heads. We are at the corner of St. George Street and I can barely see into the plaza. People are everywhere. I cannot believe this many people have come out in a show of support to make our voices heard. To say that segregation must stop.

But as I continue scanning the crowd in the fading daylight, a new realization dawns on me.

All of the people are not here to say that segregation must stop. Many of them are here to fight FOR segregation. To taunt the protestors with their "Whites Only" signs. To torment the protestors with their shouts and jeers and terrible words. To yell, to shake their fists, and to spit as the protestors try to peacefully march around the plaza.

Because some say the town plaza has past ties to the slave market, some of them are shouting taunts that have to do with that. Others are just screaming at us to know our place.

Know our place? What is our place? What is anyone's place?

Mama and Daddy and I are practically standing still now. We try to ease ourselves into the stream of people marching around the perimeter of the rectangular plaza. Mama has hold of my arm as we blend into the line and keep pace.

It is a pretty slow pace. We—the protestors—are about four or five wide as we march. From here I can now see that the crowd of people in the plaza, being wrapped by our parade of protestors, are the segregationists.

Some of them have signs, just like some of the marchers. But their signs are threatening and hateful. I try to keep my eyes forward so I do not have to see them. Of course I can still hear them. Their shouts and jeers.

I realize this is the first time I have seen this many protestors protesting our protest.

"Democracy in Action!" That is what my history teacher, Mrs. Williams, would say. I know she would get all excited and start to talk about how this was what it meant to be American! Exercising our *Right to Peaceably Assemble* and *Petition the Government for Redress of Grievances*, while another group does the same thing—only they are working against what you are working for.

It sounds like a big mess to me, but Mrs. Williams always said that was what made America different. It was what made us great. I can't help but smile a little bit. Perhaps she is right. I wonder if she is here, among the protestors.

Realizing that the people standing inside the plaza, yelling and shouting, want the exact opposite of what the line of protestors around the plaza want, makes my heart heavy.

How can an issue like that ever be solved? I go from feeling hopeful to feeling hopeless. How will things ever change when there are so many people who do not want anything to change?

How do we make them understand that giving us the same rights that they have does not diminish or take away their rights? Just because I can order lunch at the Woolworth's counter doesn't mean you cannot.

It is then that my attention is drawn to the southwest corner of the plaza. Something has happened—is happening. The crowd is going crazy as people shout and run and push and shove. Even the calm line of marchers we are part of starts to get agitated. Some people seem drawn to the commotion and chaos and move toward it, while others try to get as far away from it as possible. This creates more chaos and I am not sure what to do.

Then I feel Daddy's strong arm grab me.

Chapter 23

June 11, 1964

Mama and Daddy are sitting at the kitchen table when I come in for breakfast. I am up earlier than normal. They are reading the paper and each of them has a section.

As I sit down, Mama looks up and smiles. She asks how I slept, if I would like some breakfast, and what my plans are today. A normal sounding conversation, but Mama's voice and face aren't quite normal.

It has been a hard two days since the march at the town plaza. It was the first of the protests that we have been involved with that has turned so violent—not from the police or cattle prods, or making arrests, but from the pro-segregationists who had come to protest our protest.

They had not only yelled and spit and threatened, but they actually beat up some of the protestors. The one who was beaten the worst was a man named Andrew Young. He is not even from St. Augustine. He works with Dr. King and was here to help out. To help us organize and bring awareness to what is happening here. To lead the march.

As he tried to cross the street to the town plaza, they attacked and beat him.

I have been wondering a lot about the pro-segregationists. I wonder who they are. Like the groups protesting for civil rights, are they mothers, fathers, children? Do they work as mechanics, like Daddy? Have they served in the military like Uncle Walter? Are they students like me? Have they also lived their entire lives in St. Augustine, like me? Do they go to church? Have picnics with their neighbors?

Why is it that they have such hatred for us? I think we are probably more alike than we are different.

Why are they so opposed to treating us like they are treated? Isn't that in the Bible? Treat others as you would want to be treated.

I am pretty sure they do not want to be treated the way we are being treated. What do they think will happen if we are all treated equally?

I pick up the newspaper that Mama put down when she got up to start cooking breakfast. It is an article about Dr. King. He was back in St. Augustine yesterday. After the violence of the protest two nights ago, he held a press conference and questioned the ability of the local police to protect peaceful protestors from the violent segregationists. He also said he was here himself to be part of the protests and to be arrested if necessary.

Chapter 24

June 16, 1964

He was arrested. Martin Luther King Jr. was arrested while protesting here in St. Augustine. It was the same day that he held his press conference. Later that day he and some protestors were at the Monson Motor Lodge. It is a nice-looking motor lodge. Nice location, right downtown, facing the Castillo de San Marcos and Matanzas Bay.

Dr. King and the others were arrested when they staged a sit-in to protest that the Motor Lodge was for "whites only." That one peaceful arrest of Dr. King sure brought a lot of attention to St. Augustine. And that has brought others here to be part of our struggles.

Jackie Robinson is even here. Yes—the famous baseball player. That is where we were earlier tonight, at the St. Paul Church listening to him speak. That is not our church, but we all went anyway. Everyone—Mama, Daddy, me, Granddaddy, Grandma, and my little brother. This was the first time my brother seemed to really care about the civil rights protests and struggles. But I know that is only because it was Jackie Robinson. He loves baseball and Jackie Robinson is his hero, even though he no longer plays baseball.

There were so many people crammed into that church, we could barely breathe. We were not early enough to get seats, so we just stood in the back. It was warm, so there was a lot of fanning going on.

Jackie Robinson was great to listen to. Not Dr. King great—but great anyway. He shared some of the stories of his struggles with us—stories of the way he had been treated when he first joined the Brooklyn Dodgers. The way he was treated by other players and the fans. The stories of the abuse, the hatred, the meanness. It made me so sad.

But then he shared other stories. Stories of people who changed their mind about him when they got to know him. Stories of people who began to believe that maybe it was the talent you had and the hard work you put in that mattered, not the color of your skin .He shared stories of whites who stood up with him to demand better treatment for everyone. Those stories made me feel hopeful.

Lying here in bed, as I go over the words he spoke and the stories he told, I begin to think about the protests and marches we have had here in St. Augustine. Yes, the protestors are mainly colored people, but I am remembering that I have seen many whites also standing with us. I think of Mrs. Peabody and smile.

As I drift off to sleep, I am feeling more hopeful than I have in weeks.

Chapter 25

June 19, 1964

The hopefulness I felt two days ago has evaporated.

I am sitting in the kitchen by myself. At the table that just a little while ago was filled with breakfast dishes and people talking. Everyone has gone to start their day. I finished the dishes, but the newspaper sitting in the middle of the table draws me in like a powerful magnet.

I flip it over and once again stare at the front page pictures.

The pictures are of the Monson Motor Lodge pool. In one photo, there are about five or six young people in the pool. Some whites. Some Negros. They are huddled toward the middle of the pool. It looks like some are screaming. And Mr. Brock, the owner of the Monson Motor Lodge, is at the edge of the pool in his coat and tie and sunglasses, pouring something into the pool.

While the photos are mesmerizing to me, the article gives the most disturbing information. Mr. Brock, in an effort to get the swimmers out of the pool—these swimmers who jumped in the pool to protest that the pool was segregated—was pouring acid into the water.

I study his face in the photos. He is pouring acid into his own pool. In one photo his face looks calm while he pours, but the swimmers' faces are contorted into screams. In another photo, it is clear he is also yelling and screaming, most likely at the protestors to get out of his pool.

The article says that the protestors are activists with the SCLC, who have come to town to make trouble. It also says that there were more than a dozen rabbis, also from out of town, who held a prayer session in the parking lot just before the swimmers jumped in the pool. Apparently to cause a distraction. All of them—the rabbis and the swimmers—have been arrested.

The article gives the impression that it is all of these "outsiders" who are coming to St. Augustine that are causing this trouble. The article implies that if they would all just go back to where they came from, things here would be just fine. The article implies that the colored folks who live here in St. Augustine were all content and satisfied until these rabble-rousers started making trouble.

I set the paper down and suck in my breath. Our community was most definitely NOT satisfied with things the way they were. How is it that they can print something that is so blatantly a lie?

Why would they choose to ignore the facts? The fact that Negroes want to be treated fairly and equally. I heard it said once that the Klan controls the paper, too.

Once again I look down at the newspaper. I remember the lessons in school on the Bill of Rights and the freedom of the press. I remember the teacher telling us how important this freedom is to a democracy like ours. That the power of the press to print the truth—the facts—is the safety net that protects the people from the possible tyranny of leaders in power who believe they only need to answer to themselves.

I wonder how it is that this freedom also protects people who want to print things they know are not true.

These questions are scaring me. I stand, leave the paper in the middle of the table, and walk out of the kitchen.

Chapter 26

June 24, 1964

I am up in my room reading when I first hear the chants and the commotion and the singing. It is hard to figure out what the noise is all about. I push aside the curtain and look down the street. My eyes grow accustomed to the darkness.

In the distance I can see a mass of what could only be people. I can't clearly see the crowd, but I can see that they are moving slowly down the street. As they pass houses far down the road, I can see that those who live in those homes are turning on front lights, coming out onto porches, or looking through the windows.

I rush downstairs and I can see that everyone else also heard the commotion. The front door is open and everyone—Mama, Daddy, Granddaddy, Grandma, and even my brother—are on the porch.

Peering into the dark it is hard to clearly see the crowd. The torches they are carrying flicker in the distance as the lights slowly creep closer.

"Good Lord in heaven! It's the Klan!" My grandma's voice is nearly a whisper.

I can feel everyone on the porch tense up. Daddy steps to the edge of the porch as Mama pushes my brother back into the house. He continues to stand in the open doorway, his face reflecting the shock and fear and confusion we are all feeling.

We had heard that the local Ku Klux Klan was holding a rally downtown at the old slave market tonight. A rally designed to get the whites all worked up about our protests. A rally to demonstrate just how important protecting segregation is to them.

The local civil rights organizers said that we should all stay away. No sense in trying to protest in a situation that would only turn violent. Nonviolence is the one nonnegotiable rule for every single thing the movement stands for. So we were to all just stay away.

No one had a problem with that. What we did not expect was that they would actually bring their rally into our neighborhood.

As the crowd gets closer, I can see that what I thought was a white haze from the burning torches is really the white Klan robes that some in the crowd were wearing. Those in the Klan robes seemed to be leading the crowd. Behind them are white marchers—men, women, even some children. Some hold torches, some hold signs that support segregation laws, and a few even carry ropes.

It is clear that the purpose of the ropes is to intimidate. To make us feel fear. It is their silent way of letting us know that they are in control, they are not afraid to come into our community, and that they will use the ropes if they have to.

As the marchers draw nearer, my heart starts beating faster and my fear grows.

It is then that something miraculous happens.

I don't know where it came from, or who started it, but singing begins to emerge from the crowd of residents who have poured from their homes and stand on porches, driveways, and front lawns. It is the hymn "I Love Everybody." The song grows in volume and intensity as more Lincolnville residents join in the song being sung to the marchers on the street.

I am stunned. How can we sing such a beautiful song to such a hateful crowd?

As the marchers make their way past us on the porch, I can see the stunned faces of some of the crowd. This was apparently not the response they expected or wanted from us.

Seeing the perplexed white faces, I take a deep breath and join in the song.

Chapter 27

June 25, 1964

It is a hot, humid Florida June day as I arrive at St. Augustine Beach. It is a beautiful beach, as most Florida beaches are. This is a "whites only" beach, so I have never actually been here before. I look around at the crowds. I cannot believe how many people have shown up. There has to be hundreds of people here.

It looks like most of us are protestors, although I see pockets of people who look like they might be segregationists.

As word spread of this protest—a "wade-in," the organizers are calling it—we were also warned that emotions and frustrations are running high for those opposed to our movement. With more and more attention nationally on not just St. Augustine but the whole south, the support for a national law to guarantee everyone civil rights is growing stronger. People are saying it is only a matter of time and the law will be in place and segregation will be outlawed.

This is making those who believe in segregation desperate as they try to keep things from changing.

Forcing change is difficult, I have discovered. But I am also thinking that preventing change that is getting momentum, must be nearly impossible.

I imagine that is why we are being told that, in spite of our nonviolent commitment, those protesting against us have no such commitment and are becoming more and more frustrated, agitated, and hateful.

As I gather with a small group on the beach, one of the organizers joins us with some last-minute words of advice and encouragement. Then he is off to speak with another group.

Looking around at all of the people on the beach, it is easy to see who plans to be part of the wade-in. We are the ones dressed for the beach. Shorts, t-shirts, bare feet—some even have on bathing suits. It is not a group of only Negroes either. There are whites as part of our group. They are mostly young, like us.

Those people who are here to protest in favor of segregation are also easy to identify. They want the beach to remain for whites only and they are also standing at the ready.

Then there are the police officers scattered throughout the crowd. They are fully dressed in their uniforms; they all have on hats and are holding clubs. I am relieved they are not holding guns or cattle prods. I notice that they are state police—Florida Highway Patrol officers, not our local law enforcement.

I do not hear the command myself, but it seems we have been told to start the wade-in, because the groups begin to move down to the shore, and then begin to wade into the water as one large mass. The segregationists also begin to move toward the water, but the police officers also move into the water and form a wall between the two groups. We are on one side, they are on the other, and the police officers, some up to their thighs in water in spite of being completely dressed, are standing facing the other group.

I am stunned. They are protecting us!

As we wade further into the water, I begin to hear the shouts from the segregationists. Some of the words are vulgar and hateful, but I try to focus on the wonderful feel of the Atlantic Ocean on my legs. The feel of the sun on my face. The smell of the salt water.

I can see that there are also people standing on the beach. These people are not dressed for the beach, so they have no intention of getting into the water. I can tell some are segregationists because they are shouting and shaking their fists. Others must be reporters and journalists. They have cameras or notebooks and are furiously writing or taking pictures.

I am still trying to block out the hateful shouts coming from the other side of the line of police officers. I am trying to distract myself by imagining how wonderful it must be to come to this beach just for fun.

Not to stage a wade-in. Not to protest. Not to make a point. Simply to enjoy the beach. I can see St. Augustine Lighthouse from here and turn to watch the seagulls crossing the sky.

That is when it happens. I am not sure what exactly, but something happens because all of a sudden there is chaos and mayhem.

People running and shouting and falling. Police officers grabbing and dragging and clubbing. People pushing and hitting. We are no longer two groups of protestors divided by a wall of officers. We are one enormous mass of arms and legs and noise and violence.

I can barely see because of all the water being splashed and kicked into the air. I decide to try to get to shore. That is when my head snaps back with such force I lose my breath.

Someone has grabbed a hold of my hair and pulls me off my feet. I lose my balance and slip below the water. I try to get my legs back under me to stand up, but I am caught up in a tangle of arms and legs. As I thrash about I am able to get my head above water and take a deep breath. I manage to get my feet on the sandy bottom and stand as an arm comes out of nowhere and slams me in the face. I see sparks as the pain in my left eye takes my breath away again and I fall back once more.

This time as I surface, I come face to face with the owner of that arm. She is a middle-aged white woman shouting horrendous things at me as she tries to push me down again. I want so badly to reach out and push back, but I don't. Mustering all the strength I can, I turn and struggle and finally make it back to shore.

Chapter 28

June 26, 1965

"Are you sure you don't want any breakfast?" my grandma asks me for the third time this morning.

I am not normally a big breakfast eater, and today I really don't want anything. I think my family thinks that I don't want breakfast because I am feeling ill. But I am not. I do not feel sick, I reassure them. I just don't feel like eating.

The way they are looking at me, I know they are worried about me. My brother is sitting across the table from me and can't take his eyes off me. "You look like a boxer," he finally says.

He is referring to my black eye. It is a doozy. Yesterday it was red and puffy. Today it is an honest-to-goodness black eye.

It does look like I was in a fist fight with someone. This morning, looking in the bathroom mirror as I brushed my teeth, I was sure it was someone else looking back at me. The reflection did not in any way look like me.

In some ways, I do not even feel like myself this morning.

I do not mean because of the aches and pains that I have as a result of yesterday. And there are aches and pains. In addition to my black eye, I had quite a bloody nose yesterday. Because the nose bleeds so much, there was blood all over the shirt and shorts

I had on. That probably made it seem worse.

I do have scratches on my legs and arms and a pretty big scratch that goes from my neck down my shoulder. And then there are the bruises. I have them on my arms and legs, my jaw, and even on my foot. I think that was from someone stepping on it in the chaos in the water.

I endured a physical attack and I did not fight back. I realize now how powerful that is. I am proud of myself for not striking back when I could have. When maybe I was even justified in striking back to defend myself.

But I did not allow the violence of another to destroy my commitment to nonviolence.

I did not give over control of myself and my beliefs to someone so filled with hatred that she would attack a teenager for wanting to swim in the ocean.

I do not know what to say to my family. They look at the outside of me and see someone who took a beating.

How do I tell them that for the first time since I joined the movement, I am proud of myself. That I no longer feel like a fraud or a faker.

Daddy is reading the newspaper account of what happened yesterday and he looks up.

"Sounds like the police ended up arresting more of the segregationists for inciting violence and unlawful behavior than the protestors trying to swim." His voice has a tone of approval and satisfaction as he puts the paper down.

"Well, they were Florida Highway Patrol officers, not our local officers. I've got to believe that made a difference," Granddaddy adds as he reaches over to pick up the paper.

"The Klan did have a rally last night and seems the whites who were even touched by the police yesterday at the beach were encouraged to press charges against the police," Daddy adds.

The kitchen is once again quiet except for the sound of Mama washing dishes in the sink.

Chapter 29

July 2, 1964

It has happened. It finally happened today.

The Civil Rights Act was signed into law by the president of the United States.

Segregation is now illegal in the USA!

People have worked so hard, for so long, to get this law passed. As I sit on the front porch listening to the family watch the news report inside, I take a deep breath.

Now, if I go to the Woolworth's counter to order lunch and they refuse, it will be them breaking the law, not me.

If I want to go swimming at St. Augustine Beach again, I can do so without worrying about someone attacking me.

The city library, the golf course, the beaches—they can no longer turn us away because we are not white.

I think of these past months. This past year. I realize that this law did not get passed simply because it is a righteous law that guarantees the fair treatment everyone deserves—regardless of their skin color. If that was the case, it would have become law years ago.

It was signed into law because the people of this country let their feelings be known through peaceful protests.

Yes, because people like Martin Luther King Jr. inspired and organized. And people like Rosa Parks said enough was enough. And thousands of people across the nation banded together to challenge the unfairness of segregation laws.

But it is also being signed because of people like me. Because I sat at the lunch counter and got arrested. Because I marched and sat and showed up. Because I waded into the ocean and got beat up.

I touch my cheek, the bruise and black eye fading fast. The outward scars of these things will ultimately disappear. But the inside ones will always be part of who I now am.

With a start I realize that I am glad to have scars, both inside and out. That they attest to the fact that I was part of this.

Yes—I helped to force change!

Timeline of Historical Events

June 26, 1963–Teenagers conduct sit-ins at McCrory's, Woolworth's, and Service Drugs. In all three establishments, the lunch counters close immediately and all unoccupied seats are removed.

June 27, 1963–Sporadic picketing continues at McCrory's and Woolworth's. Lunch counters at both establishments remain closed. Henry Twine and other NAACP members appear at a City Commission meeting and ask why Negroes have been barred from the public library and city-owned golf putting course. Commissioners reply it was a misunderstanding, that the city itself is fully integrated and any remaining dispute is with private business. The commission then passes an ordinance limiting the size of signs used by pickets and prohibiting loitering or barring the entrance to any business.

July 18, 1963–Picketing in St. Augustine is reported by FBI agents to Director J. Edgar Hoover. However, just before midnight, Washington is notified of sixteen arrests at four lunch counters earlier in the day. Among them are teenagers who will come to be known as the "St. Augustine Four," who have been charged during a "sit in" at Woolworth's.

July 26, 1963–An editorial in the *Daytona Beach Morning Journal* is highly critical of the decision of Judge Mathis not to release juveniles unless they promise to refrain from picketing. It quotes a staff member of the U.S. Commission on Civil Rights as stating, "Can such a thing be true in this country?" The editorial is quickly reprinted and distributed as a flier. Six blacks are arrested for distributing literature on private property.

Aug. 28, 1963–On the very same day as the historic "March on Washington," five black students in St. Augustine enroll at a previously white school, Fullerwood Elementary. They are: Irvin Brunson, fourth grade; his brother, Billy Charles Brunson, sixth grade; his sister, Debbie Jean Brunson, second grade; Michael Coolege Robinson, fifth grade; and Gary Alonzo Robinson, first grade.

Sept. 2, 1963–For the first time, Civil Rights demonstrations are held at the Plaza de la Constitución in downtown St. Augustine. Police use cattle prods on the protesters, and twenty-seven are arrested.

Sept. 15, 1963–The Ku Klux Klan bombs the 16th Street Baptist Church in Birmingham, Alabama, killing four girls. This murderous act shocks the nation and galvanizes the civil rights movement.

Sept. 18, 1963–Civil rights leader Robert B. Hayling and three other men—James Hauser, James Jackson, and Clyde Jenkins—are brought at gunpoint to a mass rally of the Ku Klux Klan, beaten, and nearly killed.

Oct. 22, 1963–Molotov cocktails are thrown at the homes of all three black families who integrated public schools in St. Johns County earlier in the year.

Oct. 24, 1963–A twenty-four-year-old fisherman, William David Kinard, is shot in the head and killed while he and three other white men are riding through the black neighborhood of Lincolnville late at night. When struck by the bullet, the loaded shotgun Kinard is carrying discharges through the floorboard of the car.

Oct. 29, 1963–Civil rights leader Robert B. Hayling is arrested on charges of hindering an investigation into violence in connection with an incident after the funeral of William David Kinard.

Oct. 30, 1963–Earl Johnson, a Jacksonville attorney representing the NAACP, petitions the Florida Supreme Court to order the release of the "St. Augustine Four."

Nov. 4, 1963–Four white men are acquitted of charges in connection with the beating of Robert B. Hayling at a KKK rally on September 18.

Nov. 5, 1963–Five blacks in St. Augustine, including an NAACP leader and several of his relatives, are charged with murder in the October 24 shooting death of a white man, William David Kinard. They are: Goldie Eubanks Sr.; Goldie Eubanks Jr.; Richard A. Eubanks; Harold Jenkins; and Chester Hamilton. A woman, Joyce Green, is held as a material witness. None of those arrested are ever tried for the alleged crime.

Nov. 9, 1963–At Ship's Bar in St. Augustine, three white men are overheard discussing a $500 reward for the death of a local civil rights leader, dentist Robert B. Hayling. Their conversation is reported to the FBI.

Nov. 21, 1963–A cover story in *JET* Magazine declares "OLDEST CITY IN U.S. MOST BACKWARD IN RACE RELATIONS."

Nov. 22, 1963–President Kennedy is killed.

Dec. 16, 1963–A report from the St. Johns County grand jury blames recent violence on militant Negro leaders and the Ku Klux Klan. As part of an investigation orchestrated by State Attorney Dan Warren, the grand jury has heard testimony from thirty-six witnesses in five days.

Jan. 13, 1964–Sheriff L. O. Davis notifies the FBI that the whereabouts of missing witness in the William Kinard murder investigation, Joyce Green, remain unknown. Cases against Goldie Eubanks Sr. and other St. Augustine blacks charged in the shooting death of William Kinard are postponed.

Jan. 14, 1964–The state legislature of Florida orders the release of the "St. Augustine Four." The teenage protesters have been incarcerated for over five months because of their participation in a sit-in at Woolworth's lunch counter. During that time, the Sunshine State has been subjected to withering criticism in national media and outrage has been expressed in numerous other demonstrations.

Jan. 21, 1964–Charles Brunson is attending a PTA meeting at Fullerwood Elementary School in St. Augustine when his car is destroyed by a firebomb at about 8:19 p.m. He is father to three of the five black children who integrated the school nearly a year earlier.

Feb. 7, 1964–The home of Mr. Roberson on Gault Street is firebombed and destroyed. His son was among the first five black students to enroll at Fullerwood Elementary School the previous year.

Feb. 8, 1964–Hours after the Roberson house burns to the ground, four loads of buckshot are fired into the home of Dr. Robert B. Hayling at 8 Scott Street. The spray of deadly pellets just misses Dr. Hayling's pregnant wife, but kills his dog.

March 6, 1964–Dr. Hayling drives with Goldie Eubanks, Henry Twine, Roscoe Halyard, and several other NAACP members, to meet with aides of Dr. King in Orlando, at a meeting of the Southern Christian Leadership Conference (SCLC).

March 11, 1964–Robert B. Hayling, now identifying himself as a representative for the SCLC, begins recruiting assistance in New England with Hosea Williams, an aide to Martin Luther King Jr. Students from the north are being asked to participate in demonstrations in St. Augustine from March 21 through 28 and March 29 through April 4.

March 12, 1964–Mayor Joseph Shelly receives at least two phone calls alerting him to an impending "mass invasion." One is from a St. Augustine student who is attending college in New England. The other is from a Boston radio commentator. Shelly learns the mother of the governor of Massachusetts will be visiting St. Augustine and is asked what he'll do if she violates local segregation law.

March 23, 1964–About thirty students, faculty members, and chaplains from New England arrive in St. Augustine with the stated purpose of staging demonstrations.

March 28, 1964–William England, a chaplain from Yale University, and twenty-six demonstrators, most of them white northerners, are arrested in St. Augustine for trespassing and conspiracy.

March 30, 1964–Some ninety demonstrators—including Mrs. Peabody—are arrested for trespass in several different locations. Also among those arrested are Dr. Robert L. Hayling and four visitors from New England, who take seats at the Ponce de León Motor Lodge. The interracial group includes Mrs. John M. Burgess, Rev. Donald Clark, Judith Creedy, and Rev. William England.

March 31, 1964–Singing freedom songs, about 150 students from Murray High School march to the exclusive Ponce de León Hotel, entering the dining room and taking seats at tables set with linen, silverware, and glassware. In a scene which draws inevitable comparisons to Birmingham, St. Augustine police respond with cattle prods and dogs on leashes, arresting all the young protesters.

April 1, 1964–In a press release, Mayor Joseph Shelly claims members of the national press and network news outlets have "misquoted and distorted" his statements. The mayor harshly criticizes Mary Peabody, stating he deplores her actions—i.e., that the mother of a sitting governor has come to another state with the open intention of breaking the law. He also tells reporters the Civil Rights protests have generated no enthusiasm among local Negroes.

April 2, 1964–Dr. Robert Hayling and Mary Peabody appear at a hearing in U.S. District Court with co-defendants William S. Coffin and Annie Ruth Evans. Representing the Civil Rights demonstrators in federal court are attorneys John Pratt, Tobias

Simon, and William Kunstler. Mrs. Peabody testifies, posts bond, and is released.

April 13, 1964–Mary Peabody appears as a guest on the "Today" show. Leaders in St. Augustine are enraged.

April 14, 1964–Trinity Episcopal Church is integrated by five local black Episcopalians. Bishop Hamilton West has ordered all churches in the Diocese of Florida to open their doors to anyone wishing to attend services.

April 23, 1964–Protesters resume their activities in St. Augustine.

April 26, 1964–The vestry at Trinity Episcopal Church meets and drafts a resolution to Bishop Hamilton West, censuring the National Council of the Episcopal Church for its position on civil rights. The vestry members include Dr. Hardgrove Norris, E. W. Trice, Clayton Stratton, and Kenneth Barrett—as well as A. H. Tebeault, publisher of the St. Augustine Record.

May 18, 1964–Martin Luther King Jr. visits St. Augustine and characterizes the town as "a small Birmingham."

May 19, 1964–The conservative vestry at Trinity Episcopal Church votes to withhold funds from its diocese. A three-page letter blaming "racial agitators" is published in the church bulletin.

May 25, 1964–Martin Luther King Jr. returns to St. Augustine.

May 29, 1964–SCLC staffer Harry Boyte, a white aide to Martin Luther King Jr., reports to police that his parked car was shot up during the night. In addition, Boyte reports to police that the Crescent Beach safe house of King was shot up during the night. Nobody was in the house at the time of the shooting. A photo would be taken later, showing King pointing to a bullet hole in a window of the house.

May 31, 1964–FBI agents in St. Augustine report to director J. Edgar Hoover that the overwhelmed sheriff, L. O. Davis, has been deputizing members of the Ku Klux Klan to provide assistance with maintaining order in town.

June 3, 1964–During hearings regarding the ban on nighttime demonstrations in St. Augustine, Judge Bryan Simpson interrogates Sheriff L. O. Davis on the witness stand. Davis denies that Klansmen have been made special deputies.

June 5, 1964–Martin Luther King Jr. holds a press conference in St. Augustine. In his remarks, King demands that the city desegregate private businesses, hire additional black employees, establish a bi-racial committee, and drop charges against all demonstrators. King threatens to bring a "non-violent army" to St. Augustine should these demands not be met.

June 9, 1964–In his Jacksonville federal courtroom, Judge Bryan Simpson rules that the city of St. Augustine cannot legally ban demonstrations during the day or at night, thereby setting the stage for increasingly violent showdowns in the city. That night, SCLC staffer and close aide to Martin Luther King Jr., Andrew Young, would be tricked by his good friend and fellow staffer, Hosea Williams, into leading a night march to the Slave Market. During the march, Young would be assaulted twice by segregationists while trying to lead marchers across King Street to the Plaza.

June 10, 1964–Martin Luther King Jr. returns to St. Augustine and holds a press conference at the Elk's Rest. During his press conference, King asserts that he and Ralph Abernathy will take part in a demonstration and be arrested, if necessary. King also expresses concerns about local law enforcement's ability to protect demonstrators from segregationists.

June 11, 1964–For the one and only time in Florida, Martin Luther King Jr. is arrested. After polite conversation with hotel owner, James Brock, King and others are arrested for an attempted sit-in at the Monson Motor Lodge. Others who were arrested with him include Ralph Abernathy, Bernard Lee, and Clyde Jenkins.

June 16, 1964–Retired baseball player Jackie Robinson visits St. Augustine and speaks at a rally attended by 400 people at St.

Paul AME Church. While in town, Robinson invites Audrey Nell Edwards and JoeAnn Anderson, of the St. Augustine Four, to vacation at his home in Connecticut.

June 18, 1964—In what is remembered as one of the most significant events of the St. Augustine Civil Rights movement, SCLC activists Al Lingo and J. T. Johnson, along with local foot soldiers, integrate the swimming pool at the Monson Motor Lodge. Hotel owner James Brock loses his cool and pours acid into the pool to remove the integrated group of swimmers. Images of Brock pouring acid into the pool end up on front pages of newspapers worldwide.

June 18, 1964—At the same time the Monson pool is being integrated, fifteen rabbis led by Israel Dresner create a distraction in the hotel's parking lot by leading a Hebrew prayer session. All fifteen are arrested in what is still the largest arrest of rabbis in American history.

June 24, 1964—Segregationist leader Connie Lynch addresses Klansmen and other white citizens during a rally at the Slave Market. During the speech, Lynch alludes to the three missing civil rights workers in Mississippi—a remark the crowd greets with laughter.

June 24, 1964—After Lynch finishes speaking at the rally, the Ku Klux Klan holds a night march in Lincolnville. Black residents pour into the streets to greet the Klan by singing the words to the hymn, "I Love Everybody." The march takes place without incident.

June 25, 1964—Morning and afternoon wade-ins staged at "whites only" St. Augustine Beach by SCLC activists and local foot soldiers both end in violence as segregationists attack the demonstrators. Numerous arrests are made by Florida Highway Patrol troopers.

June 25, 1964—Connie Lynch is joined by Ku Klux Klan attorney J. B. Stoner to lead a rally at the Slave Market for approximately 400 white citizens. Stoner and Lynch both give hate speeches directed at blacks and Jews. Stoner encourages all white men who were hit by troopers at the beach wade-ins to press charges against police.

July 2, 1964–The Civil Rights Act is signed into law, making segregation illegal in this country!

***Source: Civil Rights Library of St. Augustine, Flagler College

http://cdm16000.contentdm.oclc.org/ui/custom/default/ collection/default/resources/custompages/home/timeline.html.

Special Thanks

I would like to express a special thank you to the following:

The Florida Humanities Council

> For providing such wonderful opportunities to learn about the history, art, and culture of our state. They work tirelessly to provide teacher trainings that put teachers and leading scholars together in order to dig beyond what is published in traditional history books.

Keith Simmons

> Who has been instrumental in facilitating these summer workshops that allow the state-wide networking of educators and historians in order to better meet the educational needs of the classroom.

Dr. Michael Butler of Flagler College

> His work with the Civil Rights Library of St. Augustine has helped to provide an abundance of resources and documents related to the events in this book.

The Florida Historical Society

> For working so diligently to preserve and honor the history of the state of Florida